social anxiety relief for teens

Practical CBT Exercises and Coping Skills to Build Confidence, Control Anxiety, and Thrive in Social Situations

jason forte

contents

Get Your Bonus Ebook Stop Limiting Yourself

+ Free Small-talk Field Guide

+ 5 Simple Secrets of Great Communicators

Scan the QR code above to claim your free bonuses

————————OR————————

visit https://gifts-jasonforte.brokentiles.co/anxiety

Get Ready to Improve all your Conversations & Build Self-Confidence!

✔Five Simple Secrets of Great Communicators. Treat these tips as your bible to improve your communication skills.

✔Free e-book: Stop Limiting Yourself. Expert advice debunks the most common limiting beliefs and forces you to get out of your own head!

✔Printable Small-Talk Field Guide, including conversation topic inventory worksheet. Never be left with nothing to say, and learn to exit a conversation gracefully.

introduction

Do you know that about one out of every three people aged 13 - 18 will experience anxiety disorder symptoms during this phase of their life? In fact, over 9% of all adolescents experience a social anxiety disorder.

If you struggle to be yourself around others or to make new friends, or if you would describe yourself as extremely shy, you're not alone. Everyone feels awkward in social situations at times.

By the end of this book, you will have the tools you need to come out of your shell and beat the negative inner thoughts at the root of social anxiety. You'll also learn coping skills to get you through the most challenging moments.

There's no one-size-fits-all approach to this, so some of the topics we cover will be extremely helpful, while others may not work for you. Don't force anything, but try to come with an open mind. If any of the concepts are emotionally intense, working through them with a parent or someone you feel comfortable getting deep with would be best.

One of the first steps to confronting anxiety is to simply talk about it with someone else. What situations fill you with dread? When do you feel so awkward you wish you could just disappear? Can you think of moments when the voice inside your head shouts terribly negative things? This book contains plenty of exercises to get to the bottom of that, but the good news is that just speaking these fears out loud will begin to chip away at their power.

Many of the exercises and techniques used are based on CBT methods. These are proven strategies to help with social anxiety, but no book will ever be a proper substitute for working one-on-one with a professional who is able to build a personal relationship with you. If you are currently working with a therapist, discuss this book with them before using it to make sure it aligns with your treatment approach.

What this book will teach you includes:

- Practical techniques to improve communication skills
- Research-backed methods to build confidence and quiet internal negative thoughts
- Exercises proven to help you cope with anxiety and regulate intense emotions

You'll learn to find your voice, handle conflicts, and navigate complex emotions. You'll also discover the power of self-care and self-acceptance.

We will explore how to find the people and activities that bring you joy. We'll talk about some options you may not have already thought of, and we'll do some exercises that will get you thinking outside the box.

Handling emotions is at the core of dealing with social anxiety, so we will explore the concept of emotional regulation and staying in control. You will learn about the main types of emotions and how to use them to your benefit.

Negative self-talk enhances anxiety, so we will learn to apply proven methods to stop a negative spiral before it gets too far.

We will also discuss how to connect more deeply with those around you and feel a sense of belonging in the community you have created.

We are social creatures, but a lot of us get in our own way when forming healthy relationships. The methods in this book will break down some of the simple barriers that might be holding you back. Not only that, but you'll gain a better understanding of your peers and be able to relate with the people around you more deeply.

The better we all communicate, the more we can all enjoy the human experience, help each other, and get the most out of life!

mindset

Before we jump into the content, a serious question: Why are you reading this book?

People do better at everything they attempt when they know *why* they are doing it.

The simple questions below should help you consider what you'd like to get out of this book. You can be superficial or go as deep as you like, but give the questions below a little bit of thought.

If you have a journal to write in, that would be great - you'll use it a lot more throughout the book. If you have already done this exercise in the *Social Anxiety Relief Workbook for Teens,* you can go back to those answers and see if anything has changed since then. Now, on to the questions:

1. What are the one or two main struggles you would like to improve when it comes to social anxiety?
2. What would happen if you continued in your current situation without making any changes?
3. What excites you most about gaining power over shyness or social anxiety?

4. List 5 strengths that have helped you overcome past obstacles. How will you use those strengths to gain social confidence?
5. What advice and words of encouragement would you give to your 8-year-old self?

1. what's the deal with social anxiety?

. . .

> *Everything will be okay in the end. If it isn't okay, it isn't the end.*
>
> — Paulo Coelho

Do you ever feel like your heart is racing and your palms are sweating at the thought of going to a party or meeting new people? Do you ever freeze up or find it impossible to keep a conversation going? You're not alone. Social anxiety is a common condition that affects millions of people. But where does it come from?

Well, it turns out the origins of social anxiety are a complex mix of genetics, environment, and the way your brain works. For instance, if you have a family history of anxiety or have gone through traumatic events, you may be more susceptible to developing social anxiety. And even the way your brain puts thoughts together can play a role. Negative self-talk and catastrophic thinking can contribute to social anxiety.

Celebrities like Zendaya, Adele, and even lifelong star Oprah Winfrey have spoken openly about their struggles with social anxiety. So if you're not naturally a social butterfly, let's start by calling out that there's nothing unusual about that and many successful people in the public spotlight are built the same way.

if we're social creatures, why is social anxiety even a thing?

"Anxiety" wasn't always a word used to describe the feeling of being stressed or nervous. In fact, it took centuries for people to understand what we now know as "social anxiety disorder."

These days, we know that social anxiety can have multiple causes. And, since it often starts in the adolescent years, experts are paying extra attention to what causes it in teens. Some of the most common factors include:

- Trouble at home
- Being bullied
- Family history of anxiety
- Negative experiences that need to be processed
- Temperament (someone is naturally prone to feeling anxious or worrying)
- Health or physical problems
- Having an outward appearance or condition that attracts attention

social anxiety disorder starts with a vengeance in teen years

There are a few reasons why this might be. For one, being a teenager can be an awkward time in general. You have many talents and unique skills, but you may not know what they are or how to recognize them yet. Your body is going through physical changes as you mature. Plus, your brain is still developing, especially the part that helps you control your emotions and make decisions. That's why there are exercises later in this book that help you become more aware of your talents and passions.

There's a lot of pressure to "be yourself", but most people at this age are still trying to figure out who they are and how they fit in. The truth is, it's fine to not know your place in the world or be confident in your abilities just yet. This kind of pressure can add to feelings of anxiety. Later on, we'll discuss how to find your people simply by gaining a better understanding of what makes you, *you*.

Our society has an unhealthy obsession with success. Do you ever avoid speaking up, trying something new, or working on an idea because you're concerned it won't be good enough? There's an unnecessary amount of attention placed on outperforming our peers or getting into the best school, getting rich or gaining likes and followers, or just achieving a certain aesthetic. It comes from all directions, and our entire society pushes us to keep being better, stronger, faster, more desirable. This is stressful! And it's putting a lot of unnecessary pressure on teenagers.

It's also possible that social anxiety disorder runs in families and was passed down through generations. When something traumatic has happened to a person, they might develop anxiety disorders and have trouble coping with situations that would not be difficult for others who have not gone through that trauma.

what social anxiety feels like

Social anxiety can make it hard to interact with others and feel comfortable in groups. You might feel like everyone is watching and judging you or that you're doing something wrong. These fears can make it hard to hang out with friends, participate in class, or even spend time with family. Does any of this sound familiar?

One of the most challenging parts of social anxiety is the negative internal dialogue that comes with it. This inner voice might constantly criticize, saying things like "You're not good enough" or "you're so cringey," or just "yikes," on repeat. These thoughts can make it hard to focus on anything else and can make you feel even more nervous and self-conscious. Do you struggle with negative thoughts? What words are going through your mind right now? Just take note of what you're thinking. We'll go into this deeper in the 7th chapter.

A lot of us find ourselves replaying conversations in our heads, thinking about how things could have gone better or worse, obsessing over what other people are thinking, even feeling embarrassed for something we said or did a long time ago. Do you ever notice these kinds of thoughts racing through your brain during quiet moments?

As intense as that is, you might be surprised to learn that almost all people feel these emotions sometimes, but they have learned to cope with them. Throughout this book, we will go over exercises that will help you address these types of feelings before they even begin. But first, a quick look at a couple of famous people who have struggled hard with social anxiety but learned to overcome it.

some famous people who struggle with social anxiety

It turns out a lot of the celebrities we see walking the red carpet or performing on stages in front of a global audience have anxiety just like the rest of us. In fact, more and more celebrities are speaking up about mental health in general, especially when it comes to social anxiety.

Why is this a good thing? Well, first of all, it helps break the stigma around anxiety. A lot of people, even ones who perform in front of crowds for a living, have a hard time in social situations. But they have learned how to take power into their own hands. It shows that anxiety doesn't have to control anyone.

Adele

This wildly successful singer-songwriter and Grammy-winning artist has been in the spotlight for over a decade, and she still struggles with anxiety. Especially when it comes to performing in front of large crowds. Adele has openly talked about times when it got so bad that she had to leave the stage mid-performance to throw up.

Adele has been proactive in seeking therapy to help her manage her anxiety. Even though her struggles have been intense at times, she did the hard work of therapy, inner work, and finding clever ways to beat her anxiety. Did you know that Adele idolizes Beyonce as one of her role models? Despite her own successful career, Adele looks up to another singer who is just as famous as her. Adele has told reporters that when she's having an intense moment on stage, she imagines what Beyonce would do and it calms her down.

Zendaya

Actress Zendaya is a great example of someone who has been open about her struggles with anxiety and how she's been able to overcome them to be successful. She has spoken openly about how anxiety affected her in the past, especially during her teenage years. Zendaya revealed she had a hard time talking to people and was often very self-conscious about her appearance, but she pursued her passion for acting anyway.

She has learned to manage her anxiety by focusing on her goals, taking care of herself and her mental health, and surrounding herself with positive people. She also made sure to seek help when she needed it, whether it was talking to friends and family or seeing a therapist.

Her honesty and openness can inspire anyone who may be going through some of the same feelings. It shows that even successful people can have anxiety and that it is possible to overcome it with the proper support and mindset.

Oprah Winfrey

Oprah has been interviewing other famous people for almost 40 years, and despite her immense success, she still deals with anxiety. Oprah used to struggle to talk to some people. She found herself feeling extremely awkward and insecure. She had some awful experiences in her childhood, including abuse. Still, she did not let that define her and relentlessly pursued the career no one believed she could have. Oprah powered through her social anxiety by doing what terrified her most.

key takeaways

- Social anxiety has affected people since ancient times, but we have only just begun to learn why it occurs and how to make it easier to deal with.
- Many factors contribute to the onset of social anxiety in the teenage years.
- Social anxiety is a common condition, and many celebrities are open about their struggles to overcome it

2. skills for a thriving social life

. . .

 People will forget what you said and did, but they will never forget how you made them feel.

— Maya Angelou

Now that we've covered what it feels like to have social anxiety, and that it is pretty typical for teens to struggle in this area, let's take the first steps toward overcoming it. A lot of what's behind social anxiety has to do with self-confidence. This chapter will build a foundation by covering some practical skills that will make social interactions easier.

Imagine if you didn't have to worry about what someone was thinking because you *know for a fact* that you're not being awkward or violating some social norm. By focusing on a few social skills, you can take the focus off of you and place it on the people around you. By learning to engage with people in a way that makes them comfortable, you can alleviate yourself of some of the pressures that many people with social anxiety face.

You may already possess these skills and this chapter may be a breeze. So, what's the point? By making sure the basics are all covered, you can enter every situation with a higher level of confidence. Let's go!

communication skills

Being able to effectively communicate with others is crucial for building and maintaining relationships. This includes the ability to speak your mind clearly, listen actively, and respond appropriately to the thoughts and feelings of others. It also involves reading nonverbal cues like body language, facial expressions, and tone of voice.

Making eye contact is a crucial skill, but it can be uncomfortable for people who feel nervous or insecure in a situation. While it might not feel natural, maintaining eye contact is important to establish trust and get a good conversation flowing.

People tend to avoid eye-contact when they are lying, or when they are angry, hurt, or disgusted by the person they are speaking to. So, if we don't look at someone when we speak to them, it can be confusing to them.

Here are some tips to help when you find it difficult to make eye contact:

- Follow the 50/70 rule. When you are speaking, try to maintain eye contact 50% of the time. When you are listening, try to maintain eye contact 70% of the time. (Be careful not to become overly mathematical with this; it's simply a general rule.)
- Try to maintain eye contact for around five seconds at a time as an additional tactic. After a brief moment of casual side-glancing, start making eye contact again.
- Try to move your eyes slowly when you glance away.

Interpreting Body Language is tricky because it is dependent on the context of the situation, someone's personality, and cultural differences. The best way to get better at understanding nonverbal communication is to observe people around you.

Imagine your teacher and your parent are speaking behind a window. You can see them, but you can't hear anything they say. By observing the body language and facial expressions, you can get a pretty good idea of whether the conversation is positive or if trouble is brewing.

Body language and facial expressions—the things we don't say out loud—can reveal a lot about our thoughts and feelings. In fact, up to 60% of what a person says is expressed through nonverbal language. Learning how to read body language in others is a skill, but you also need to understand what your own nonverbal communication is actually saying.

Want to learn how to read body language better? Becoming more aware of your surroundings is a great start:

1. Be very observant. Start by becoming more aware of the nonverbal cues people use as they communicate. Are their shoulders tense or relaxed? Are their arms by their side, moving frantically, or crossed in front? What can their facial expression tell you, especially if you can't hear what they're saying? Casually observe people in public and see if you can figure out what they're thinking or feeling.
2. Put together the pieces of an unfamiliar situation. Next time you go to a store or restaurant, pay close attention to how things work. What do the employees' uniforms say about the jobs they do? Is there a hierarchy? Can you tell who is in charge and who would be the best person to ask for assistance if you needed something? Observe how they interact. Does anyone seem particularly happy, stressed, grouchy, or helpful?
3. Learn what is expected, depending on the situation. Every environment has its own unspoken rules about how people are expected to behave. Try to figure out these rules by paying attention to the subtle cues people give off. For example, how do people act in line at the grocery store versus at a birthday party? Or in class versus in the lunchroom?
4. Vibe check. It's important to match the mood and energy of the people in a room. When you enter a new social situation, pick

two people and observe how they act. Watch their facial expressions, the gestures they make with their hands and arms, and the tone of their voice. What does this tell you about the mood in this setting? Is it serious or playful? Quiet or full of excitement? We are likely to draw attention when we enter a new environment, so being able to read the room will let you know how to best match the energy.

listening—really listening

Active listening is one of the most important communication skills a person can master. It is all about asking questions, expressing interest, and making sure everyone understands each other.

Learning to be a great active listener will put you at an advantage in every situation. By listening, you'll make a great impression without even needing to say much. A person feels important and validated when someone is interested enough to listen to them.

Also, by listening actively, you always know what is going on in any situation. Being this aware of your surroundings makes it easier to say things that will be interesting to the group.

Can you remember ever being taught to listen? In our childhoods, we are commanded "Listen!" by parents, teachers, and other authority figures. But listening—I mean, truly listening—is a difficult skill to teach and it requires practice.

You will not always be a great active listener, and you don't always need to be! The best way to start is to focus on the most important conversations. Everyone is different, so the ways you show you are listening might be different from someone else.

These are the main things to do when you want to actively listen:

- Put your phone away, turn off any distractions, and pay full attention to the person you are speaking with.
- Focus your attention on what the person is saying, don't get distracted by your thoughts or what you plan to say next.

- Pay attention to nonverbal cues. What does their tone of voice tell you? How about their facial expressions and body language?
- Before replying to what the person is saying, ensure you understand what they meant.
- If you don't fully understand what they meant, ask a clarifying question ("what do you mean by that?" for example).
- Sometimes it feels easiest to pretend we understand something, but by politely interrupting with a simple question, you can make sure you understood.

mirroring: listen and learn

I'm about to give you an easy way to ask a clarifying question. It's as simple as repeating back what someone has just said, like holding up a mirror to their statement. Use this tactic when you want to question something but don't know quite what to say.

How about times when you feel frozen and can't come up with the words to keep a conversation going? You can use this tactic to buy yourself time while showing you're interested but keeping the focus on the other person.

This is a great way to invite someone to tell you more, and you barely have to do any of the work. Mirroring can keep tough conversations friendly, plus the only skill it relies on is your tone of voice. Let's take look at a couple examples:

Mirroring a friend

One of your friends says to you, "Why do you hang out with them? They are so boring."

You don't agree with your friend's opinion, but you're not sure how to react and don't want to argue. So, you repeat back the last thing they said, in the form of a question. You say, "they are so boring?"

By repeating exactly what your friend said back to them, you're making them think harder about their words. They subconsciously feel the need to explain what makes this other group of people so boring. Maybe they think harder and decide they are being rude.

See, you didn't disagree with your friend's opinion, but you gave them a chance to examine what they just said.

You didn't agree either, so you've taken the first step to standing your ground.

Mirroring made easy

The thing about mirroring is that most people will never realize you are doing it. Here's a trick to try out y0ur mirroring skills in an easy situation. Imagine this:

You're in the car on the way home from school. Your mom says, "make sure to get all your homework done and then clean up all that mess".

Reply nicely, like you're curious: "clean up all that mess?" and watch what happens. I would bet money that she starts to explain what mess she's talking about. Maybe it's dishes you left in the sink, maybe it's dirty clothes on the floor of your room - whatever it is, she will probably start to tell you a lot more about it.

Why? Because you showed her you were listening and asked politely, using her exact words. Even if you know the answer, try the mirroring technique just to get comfortable with how to control your tone and use it naturally.

Look out for any moments at home or with close friends where you could easily sneak in a question just by repeating the last few words someone just said. Watch how people open up and start to explain exactly what they meant.

This is a powerful tool to help communication flow better, but it's important to mention that your tone of voice and facial expressions need to be friendly and relaxed for this to work. If you are able to mirror someone in a nice way, they will feel invited to share more about their opinion. However, if it's done with a bad attitude, it will not be effective. If this sounds interesting (or confusing), I'd suggest checking out the Chris Voss video about *mirroring* on YouTube. He used to be an FBI hostage negotiator and he explains how he used this technique to deal with some of the toughest criminals in the world.

showing empathy

Would you believe me if I told you there's an upside to experiencing anxiety? The ability to understand and share the feelings of others is key to building strong relationships. People who have gone through the struggles of anxiety are usually way better at relating to other peoples' pain or hardship.

Imagine you get to school and your friend is being quiet, ignoring you, and generally acting weird. You might feel hurt. Maybe you're annoyed they're treating you like this. It feels like they might be mad at you, so it's natural if you take it personally. But if we back up and consider the alternatives before getting upset, everyone wins.

Showing empathy looks like this: we put in an effort to understand our friend in this moment. Did something happen this morning that put them in a bad mood? Is something bothering them? There's no way to know unless we approach with empathy and try to learn.

Here's a little exercise to do with at least one other person. This helps the participants learn how different people react to emotions or situations, and it emphasizes how we all experience events differently:

1. Gather a set of index cards or post-it notes.
2. On each card, write down a different emotional state or situation, such as "feeling anxious," "feeling lonely," or "dealing with a breakup."
3. Take turns drawing a card and imagining what it would feel like to be in that emotional state or situation.
4. Each person writes down their thoughts and feelings about the situation.
5. Also write how you would act: do you want to be left alone? Would you rather talk it out with a friend?

6. The person who drew the card shares their reaction first. Then, go around the circle so everyone else shares how they would react too.
7. Pay close attention to how differently each person feels and acts in the same type of situation.
8. Reflect on what you have learned about each other and how different people can have totally different responses to the same kind of situation.

Since you know what it is to suffer through anxiety, you will likely find it easier to empathize with others, no matter what it is they are going through. Empathy and compassion rely more on your nature than any social skills.

problem solving

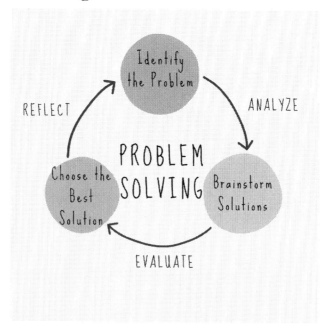

Knowing how to handle conflicts is crucial for managing any challenges that come your way. Problem-solving is a valuable skill that allows you to break down issues, weigh your options and make good choices. Developing this skill will also make you more self-sufficient and able to bounce back when things get tough.

Problem solving is a simple concept on its own, but it can be used to work with complex issues. The process looks like this:

- Step one is to identify the problem. Is there a problem at all? If so, what is it and why do we care about it?
- Step two is to analyze. Who does the problem affect? Why is it a problem?
- Step three is to brainstorm solutions. If this is a group discussion, give everyone an equal voice in proposing ideas. If this is a problem you are solving on your own, keep an open mind and think outside the box for potential solutions.
- Step four is to evaluate the ideas you or the group has come up with. Are there any ideas that would definitely not work? Why not? The aim is to make the best choice for everyone involved.
- Step five is to choose and implement the best solution.

If the problem is now solved, great! You're done. More complex problems might need another round of processing, though. So if the problem still exists, reflect back on what worked and what didn't work. Then go through the process again using what you learned from the first time.

Here's an example. You and your friend disagree about what to do on the weekend. You want to go to the movies, but your friend wants to go bowling. Let's look at a healthy problem-solving technique in action:

1. Identify the problem: You and your friend have different priorities.
2. Analyze the problem: Listen actively and try to understand your friend's perspective. You might ask your friend, "What is important to you about going bowling this weekend?" Express

your own feelings about why you want to go to the movies, too.

3. Brainstorm possible solutions together: You and your friend suggest different options. Maybe it works to go see the movie first, and then bowling later that day. Maybe it makes sense to go bowling this weekend and the movies next weekend.

4. Evaluate what makes the most sense. You can consider your budget, how much time you have, and anything else that affects the decision.

5. Choose the best solution: You two pick the option that works best for both of you.

6. Reflect on the experience: Did this go smoothly? Was the decision fair? Were you both happy in the end? Think about if anything could be improved for next time.

By following this emotionally healthy problem-solving technique, you expressed your own feelings in a calm and non-confrontational way. You actively listened to your friend's perspective and voiced your own opinion. You worked together to find a fair solution. This approach can help you positively navigate conflicts and build stronger relationships.

self-awareness and self-regulation

Self-awareness is the ability to understand your own thoughts, feelings, and actions. It allows you to recognize your strengths and understand how your emotions and actions affect you and the people around you. When you gain insight into yourself and your behaviors, it is easier make decisions about how to respond to different situations.

Self-regulation, on the other hand, is the ability to control your thoughts, feelings, and actions. This is the skill allows you to control your emotions; not let your emotion control you. Self-regulating allows you to manage your emotions and impulses. You make deliberate choices about how to behave because you recognize the power you have over your emotions.

Together, self-awareness and self-regulation help build emotional intelligence. They will allow you to navigate the complex social and emotional landscape of your teenage years more effectively, setting you up for success in the future.

Self-awareness and self-regulation are complex concepts, and we will explore them in more detail in chapter 5.

Are there some skills mentioned in this chapter that you've already got a handle on? By developing those skills further, you will be better equipped to navigate social interactions with your peers and adults, build positive relationships, and communicate effectively.

It may be frustrating at first if any of these skills don't seem to come naturally. It's important to remember that nothing changes overnight, and we develop and improve these communication skills for our entire life.

The best way to make a big change is to start small. Notice areas for improvement and try to make tiny adjustments. Chase progress, not perfection.

key takeaways

- Communication skills are about so much more than just the words we speak.
- Listening actively is just as important as speaking clearly.
- Use "mirroring" when you don't know what to say but want to keep the conversation moving.
- Empathy and problem-solving techniques help us understand those around us and get along better with them.
- Self-awareness is about knowing yourself: your thoughts and feelings make sense, so your actions make sense too.
- Self-regulation is about knowing you can control your thoughts feelings and actions.

3. coping skills for anxiety (and life in general)

· · ·

 Don't quit. Suffer now and live the rest of your life a champion.

— Muhammad Ali

In this chapter, we will discuss the uncomfortable feelings associated with social anxiety and the reasons behind them. This gives you the tools to recognize when anxiety is taking hold.

We will also get into the concept of automatic thoughts, how they can lead to a downward spiral, and how to stop that spiral before it goes too deep.

By the end of this chapter, you will have gained a better understanding of social anxiety and some coping skills to help you gain control over it.

Emotional and mental symptoms of social anxiety can make you feel just as bad on the inside as on the outside. When you have social anxiety, you might feel extra self-conscious around other people. You might also constantly worry about how others see you and think about the worst possible outcome.

Here are some common ways social anxiety can manifest emotionally and mentally:

- Feeling like you might be judged or rejected because of how you act around others
- Being nervous about saying or doing something embarrassing
- Feeling self-conscious around people in positions of authority
- Being worried that others can tell you're uncomfortable
- Feeling too shy to speak up or start conversations because you're scared of sounding pushy or dumb
- Feeling extra nervous or overjoyed after getting compliments or applause
- Doing whatever it takes avoid being the center of attention
- Feeling scared about social situations before they even happen
- Feeling embarrassed or inferior during social interactions
- Ruminating and being embarrassed about something you did or said in the past

Since social anxiety can cause a range of uncomfortable emotions and thoughts, a typical response to these feelings is to avoid certain situations.

Do you ever avoid a situation altogether, so you don't have to deal with those emotions? If so, that's understandable. Some of the most common things avoided by people with social anxiety include:

- Events or intimate meetings with strangers
- Interactions with authorities
- Meeting new people in situations where communication is expected
- Answering the phone
- Asking for help in stores
- Interviews for school
- Giving a presentation, putting on a show in front of an audience, addressing a big crowd of friends, family, or strangers
- Family reunions that include more distant relatives

- Meetings with people they have known in the past, like former schoolmates, coworkers, etc.
- Dating or any circumstance that allows for more intimate interpersonal interactions
- Negative commentary or personal criticism in online spaces

It's pretty standard for people to avoid things that cause distress. The bad news is it actually makes anxiety much worse as time goes on. Wondering how? Because by avoiding a situation you expect to be awful, you reinforce the idea to your brain that it must be terrible. It allows anxiety to win over reality.

But when you confront the situation, even if it goes badly, your brain automatically adapts how it views that situation in the future. By showing your brain that an anxiety-inducing moment is not physically dangerous, your mind's powers of logic are able to break through your anxiety and prove it wrong.

rewiring the fear response

In a nutshell, anxiety produces fear. When our brain senses fear, it instinctually prepares us to face physical danger. So, anxiety has a sneaky way of tricking your brain into thinking an intimidating situation might actually cause you physical harm. By confronting that fear and exposing yourself to situations that make you anxious, you can prove to your primal mind that it's not as serious as it seems.

When I was younger, I was super shy. I never approached anyone at school except for a few friends, and I clung to them. I hated going into the store, I rarely participated in class, and giving a presentation was the worst thing I could imagine. One of my teachers actually thought I couldn't read well because I was so shaky when asked to read part of our textbook out loud to my class.

By the time I got to high school, I had developed a habit of avoiding conversations because I couldn't stand the thought of being the center of attention in a group of people. I knew them from school, but I didn't know them *like that.* Even if I was invited into a conversation by someone, I usually said something awkward and left the situation as quickly as I could.

Every time I avoided getting into the conversation, I reinforced the idea that I would have embarrassed myself. In reality, I was already embarrassing myself because people wanted to involve me, but I refused to participate. I thought I was being shy, but it turns out my classmates thought I didn't want to be associated with them. They thought I was acting superior which shocked me because I felt so unimportant compared to them.

Avoidance leads to missing out on experiences and opportunities that could bring joy and fulfillment. It becomes easier to justify missing out on these types of events the longer we do it. Some people convince themselves of something like "College isn't for me" because they find the application process too intimidating. Or say, "I'm not interested in dating; I'm happy alone," not because it's true, but because the thought of talking to someone they are attracted to is terrifying. When we make excuses to avoid potential failure or rejection from something that would genuinely make us happier, that's a problem.

It is normal to justify our actions (or inaction) but the truth is, we are selling ourselves short and letting our fears control our lives if we fall into the habit of avoiding things that stress us out.

In a break from all that intensity, the good news is it's easy to overpower avoidance by taking tiny steps. By learning some coping skills, it will be easier to gather the courage and confidence that makes tough situations manageable.

automatic thoughts, a chain reaction of anxious feelings

Let's now focus on understanding some of the root causes of the fears that come with social anxiety. There are a few things our brain automatically starts doing that can make anxious situations worse.

Automatic thoughts are the little voice in your head that you don't always know is there. Sometimes these thoughts can be harmful and make you anxious or upset. They can be especially loud when you're in a situation that already causes stress. For example, if you're nervous around people and you're invited to a party, you might have thoughts like "I won't fit in" or "Everyone will think I'm weird."

By learning to recognize and challenge these automatic thoughts, you can manage your anxiety and all the emotions and behaviors that come with it.

The diagram on the next page walks through the process. Below is more detail on how to start:

- **Listen to your thoughts:** Start by paying attention to the thoughts that go through your mind regularly. Pay close attention to the words your brain forms when you're zoned out and not distracted. Keep an eye out for common themes, the things you tell yourself repeatedly throughout the day.

- **Spot the automatic thoughts:** Once you have a sense of your common thought patterns, start to look for automatic thoughts. These thoughts happen quickly, often in response to a specific trigger or situation. They might make you doubt your skills, question your worth, and wonder if you belong.

- **Write it down:** Keeping a journal or writing down your automatic thoughts makes it easier to recognize and challenge them. It may be a little shocking to read back the words that automatically go through your mind. Look at what you've written and ask yourself: would you speak to a friend the same way your mind speaks to you? Most of us would never be as mean to a friend as we are to ourselves. Many people struggle with negative self-talk, so it is important to expose those useless thoughts and challenge them.

- **Check the evidence:** Once you have identified an automatic thought, just examine it. Is there any evidence that supports it? Does thinking this thought protect you from potential harm in any way? Or is this negative belief just your inner saboteur talking down to you? Challenging where this thought came from can help you see it objectively and determine whether it is realistic.

- **Challenge and modify the thought**: Once you have examined the evidence for your automatic thought, try to challenge and modify it. This may involve questioning the thought or coming up with an alternative, more realistic thought. For example, instead of thinking, "I'll do something cringey in front of everyone," you might try thinking, "I might be uncomfortable when I get to the party, but if I do something awkward, it won't be the end of the world."

- **Take Action:** Finally, take action to help prepare yourself and stay in control. If you're nervous about a party, you could coordinate to ride together with a friend so you've got a buddy from the moment you walk in. It's always a great idea to do some mental preparation before an anxiety-inducing event. We will cover a few exercises to reduce anxiety throughout this book - I would suggest trying out different methods each time you know you're going into a difficult situation.

Challenging automatic negative thoughts takes a lot of practice and it won't always be easy. It's important to keep in mind that these thoughts are normal, and everyone has them. Exercises like this can interrupt the negative cycle and help you learn to manage anxiety more effectively.

Sometimes managing negative thoughts takes more than just working through it on your own. Speaking to a therapist or counselor is always recommended if you can't get out of a negative loop. They will be able to suggest personalized solutions that fit your personality and situation.

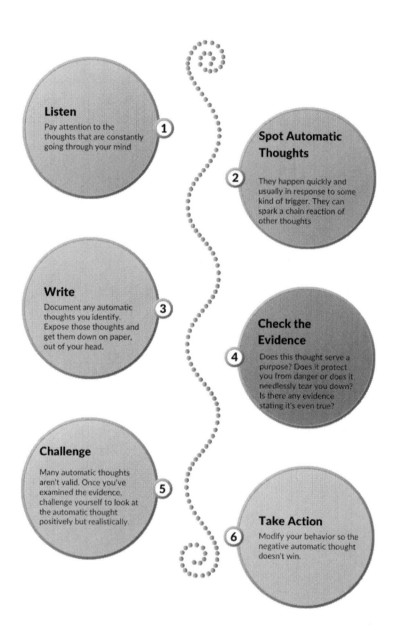

Listen
Pay attention to the thoughts that are constantly going through your mind

(1)

Spot Automatic Thoughts
(2) They happen quickly and usually in response to some kind of trigger. They can spark a chain reaction of other thoughts

Write
Document any automatic thoughts you identify. Expose those thoughts and get them down on paper, out of your head.

(3)

Check the Evidence
(4) Does this thought serve a purpose? Does it protect you from danger or does it needlessly tear you down? Is there any evidence stating it's even true?

Challenge
Many automatic thoughts aren't valid. Once you've examined the evidence, challenge yourself to look at the automatic thought positively but realistically.

(5)

Take Action
(6) Modify your behavior so the negative automatic thought doesn't win.

fight / flight / freeze response

Imagine being an ancient human who stumbles upon a wolf in the woods. You're scared for your life, and you've got a split second to figure out how to survive this encounter. Sound intense? That's the feeling at the root of anxiety, which is why it has so much power over us until we learn to control it.

A fight or flight response happens to your body when you feel like you're in danger. It's an instinctual reaction that's meant to help you protect yourself. When this happens, your body releases chemicals like cortisol and adrenaline that help you get ready to either fight the danger or run away from it. Your body goes through some physical changes too. Your heart rate and blood pressure increase, your pupils get bigger, and your muscles get ready to move. This helps you to be more alert and focused, so you can make quick decisions and react to the danger. Adrenaline taps into strength you wouldn't normally have.

A third response is called the freeze response. This happens when you are completely overwhelmed or feel powerless in the face of danger. When this happens, your body becomes really still and you might feel limp, numb or disconnected. You might even feel like you're not really there. It feels like total helplessness.

Knowing how to control your body's reaction to stress and anxiety is important, so it doesn't get too overwhelming. The first steps to managing anxiety are to get your body to a generally calmer baseline. When people are calmer in general, their reactions to anxiety can feel less intense. Here are some exercises to work on in your free time that can help keep your mind generally calmer:

Deep breathing

Deep breathing is a simple but extremely effective relaxation technique that can help to calm the body and mind. A great thing about this exercise is you can do it regularly on your own time, but you can also tap into it to stay calm when you're on the spot.

To practice deep breathing in a quiet place:

- Find a comfortable seated position and put one hand on your chest and the other one on your stomach.
- Close your eyes.
- Breathe deeply through your nose, filling your lungs and allowing your stomach to expand.
- Breathe out slowly through your mouth, allowing your stomach to relax back towards your spine.
- Repeat this several times, focusing on the breath and letting any other thoughts or worries fade into the background.

If you're in a crowded place, or you're suddenly in the spotlight and getting overwhelmed, you can do the same basic thing, just less obvious. The point of deep breathing in a stressful situation is to use a natural trick to calm your brain. Fast, shallow breathing makes us more anxious, but taking slow, deep breaths can trick our brain into calming our system down. Try it like this:

- Stay just as you are, but straighten your posture a little bit
- Observe your breath. Are your breaths shallow and fast? Or deep and controlled? Just notice for now.
- Breathe in quietly and deeply through your nose and let your lungs fill with air.
- Breathe out quietly and slowly through your nose or your mouth, whatever feels best to you
- Notice your heartbeat in your chest - feel it begin to slow down
- Notice any changes in how your head feels, if your skin tingles, and if your eyes feel more able to relax
- Enjoy this feeling of chillness; it is a natural response to deep breathing.

Progressive muscle relaxation

This exercise tenses and relaxes various muscular groups in the body, beginning with the feet and working up to the head. To practice progressive muscle relaxation:

- Put on some music, or watch something that makes you feel calm
- Lie down or sit in a comfortable position and take a few deep breaths.
- Notice your forehead - does it feel tense or relaxed? Take a deep breath in, tense it like you're incredibly surprised, and hold it for a few seconds.
- Release the tension as you exhale. Observe how your forehead feels now as its muscles continue to relax.
- Now, notice your eyes and nose. Shut your eyes tight and squeeze. Scrunch up your nose. Breathe in and hold this tension for a few seconds.
- Exhale and release the tension.
- Move on to your mouth and jaw: Tense them as you breathe in, and release them as you breathe out. Notice your facial muscles relaxing and tension fading away.
- Now move to your shoulders. We carry a lot of tension here, so take an extra deep breath.
- Tense your shoulders, moving them up your neck and getting them as close to your ears as possible. Hold for a few seconds
- Exhale deeply as you release your shoulders back down. Wiggle them and loosen everything up again.
- Repeat the process until you have worked through all of the major muscles in your body. Next are your forearms and hands. Then move to your abdomen, glutes, thighs, calves, and finally, your feet.

How did this work for you? Do you notice a difference in your mood or energy level? In which muscle group did you feel the most tension? Muscle relaxation works better for some people than others. Still, this exercise should help release some of the stress that physically manifests in your muscles.

visualization as an antidote to social anxiety

Visualization can be a powerful tool in managing social anxiety. In this exercise, you will be envisioning yourself in a situation that you would typically worry about, such as giving a presentation or attending a social event, and then mentally rehearsing (or imagining) that you did a great job.

By creating a mental image of yourself handling the situation confidently, you can reduce the anxiety you associate with that situation. Practice this enough and it can retrain your brain to see things differently.

The more specific you can be about what causes your anxiety in the situation, the more powerful the exercise will be at conquering those thoughts. For instance, if you're imagining giving a presentation to your class, visualize *exactly* what makes you anxious about that. Will your classmates make faces at you while you speak? Are you afraid of stuttering or freezing up in front of everyone? Get as detailed as you can so the situation is realistic in your mind.

Consider this: Worry is not rooted in reality. It is just a prediction of the future that imagines the worst possible outcome. It is just as valid to create a different imaginary scenario with a positive outcome instead. Both are imaginary, so what's the point in allowing the negativity to get all the attention? This is where challenging your automatic thoughts comes in. Once you practice recognizing your automatic thoughts, you can use visualization to help morph your imagination into a more positive place.

Here's an example of a visualization exercise you could try:

- Close your eyes and take a few deep breaths (deep breaths are the beginning of almost all these exercises. This is really the most effective way to calm your mind and get it prepared to work)
- Imagine yourself in a situation that makes you anxious. Visualize all the details.

- Now imagine yourself nailing it. You're confident. You understood the assignment; everyone loves it. Maybe you mess up a word here and there, but you make a joke about it and everyone laughs along with you.
- Be realistic, but don't be afraid to imagine slightly absurd scenarios. You're alone in your head and no one is watching, so it's fine to be a little over the top with your imaginary success.
- Imagine yourself in front of all those people, speaking clearly and confidently, making eye contact with the audience, and feeling comfortable and in control.
- Imagine the positive feedback and reactions of others. Again, try to imagine outrageously positive praise at first. Laugh at the words you imagine people saying to you. Think of the most over-the-top thing you've ever heard and imagine a crowd of people yelling this to you.
- Take a deep breath and let the visualization fade away.

Repeat this exercise often - it works best with a lot of practice. Be silly at first until you're able to do it without cringing. You might need to break the ice with yourself before your inner dialogue allows this positive imaginary scenario to be taken seriously. The more you practice, the easier it will be to visualize realistic scenarios that will help you to build confidence and reduce anxiety.

Remember, the anxiety we get when worrying about a future situation comes from the dark side of our imagination, so this exercise is just using the same part of our brain in a different way.

physical activities that help you get out of your head

Physical activity has been proven to reduce stress, improve mood, and increase feelings of general well-being. Some exercises that can help manage social anxiety include:

- **Cardio**: Cardiovascular exercises, such as running, cycling, or swimming, can help to reduce stress and improve mood. Some mindfulness experts consider cardio a form of active meditation because it helps your thoughts to flow with limited mental distraction, but the physical activity does not allow you to dwell on any one thing for too long.

- **Dance:** Learning a dance style is great for putting you in touch with your body, getting out of your head, and facing insecurities head-on. Ever considered salsa? Modern dance? Acrobatics? Anything that gets your body working together with your mind will help put you in a generally happier state.

- **Yoga:** Yoga combines physical movement with mindfulness and breathing techniques, which can help reduce stress and improve relaxation. You learn about the brain-body connection and how your muscles work together. You can leave a yoga class feeling very in tune with your body, and more confident in your ability to control it.

- **Strength training:** Strength training can help to build confidence and reduce stress by increasing feelings of accomplishment and self-esteem. Lifting weights and testing your strength is a great way to blow off steam.

- **Drama:** This tackles some major anxiety triggers. You'll tap into your creative side and get active in a safe space. Actors learn skills that make them great communicators, confident in front of a crowd, and able to cope with anxiety.

- **Improv Comedy:** While the thought of doing improv is probably one of the more terrifying suggestions, the skills this teaches are insanely valuable for social skills. Improv teaches us to think quickly and be witty. It relies on everyone supporting the other person because the goal of the whole group is to make the audience laugh. It's incredibly effective at improving social skills, even for extroverts.

- **Team sports:** Joining a sports team can be a great way to develop social skills and feel more comfortable in social situations. Not only do you develop athletic skills, but this is a social situation that requires more action instead of strict socialization. Joining a team inserts you into a group of people with at least one common interest and opens up opportunities to join in events with a group of people you already know.

By finding activities you enjoy, you are more likely to stick with them and experience the benefits over time. This can help build resilience and manage the discomfort associated with social anxiety.

Everyone deals with social anxiety to some extent, so it helps to get familiar with the discomfort.

Feeling nervous or self-conscious in social situations is normal, but it can become intense and constant for some people. It can make it hard to be around groups of people or in new places. But the good news is, there are things you can do to manage it.

Social anxiety is something that can be changed, and it's important to be able to lean on your friends and family. It's not a sign of weakness, and it doesn't have to hold you back. By learning healthy coping skills and not giving in to avoidance, social anxiety can be controlled.

Key Takeaways

- The symptoms of severe anxiety are comparable to situations where one feels threatened with physical injury.
- Automatic thoughts can be part of a chain reaction of anxious feelings, as they often lead to negative emotions and behaviors.
- Recognizing and challenging automatic thoughts to interrupt this chain reaction and manage anxiety is important.
- Using a few techniques like deep breathing, progressive muscle relaxation, and visualization can help you confront negative automatic thoughts and the fight or flight response
- Physical activity is just as important for mental health as it is for physical fitness

- The best way to relieve social anxiety is to become familiar with the discomfort. Exercises in this chapter help to calm you down, and we'll explore more ways to embrace the discomfort in the next few chapters

4. the six basic emotions and why they matter

. . .

> *Turning feelings into words can help us process and overcome adversity.*
>
> — Sheryl Sandberg

There are numerous forms of emotions that influence how we live and interact with others. The emotions we experience at any particular time influence the decisions we make, the actions we take, and the way we perceive what is going on around us. We may feel powerless over our emotions at times, but the better we understand them, the more we can control them.

Psychologists have attempted to categorize the various sorts of emotions that people feel. Several theories have evolved to categorize the emotions that we experience, and there is still a lot of debate over how many base emotions exist. For our purposes, I will refer to the theory of psychologist Paul Eckman. The six basic emotions he claims to be shared by all humans are happiness, surprise, sadness, anger, disgust, and fear. Let's briefly go over these basic emotions and their purpose.

Happiness: the greatest positive emotion that we all have. It is associated with contentment and pleasure, and it is closely related to our psychological well-being and health.

Why it matters: This emotion helps us feel a sense of purpose or belonging. It is theorized that happiness evolved to help humans adapt to survive by teaching us to seek out positive experiences. People who identify as happy are able to attract others more easily and activities that bring them joy, have higher energy levels, and are more resilient in the face of adversity.

Surprise: A physiological state that occurs as a result of an unexpected incident. It could be beneficial, but surprise can also be neutral or negative. The surprise of hearing you'll get a pop quiz versus the surprise of noticing your best friend across the street is the same emotion with a very different response.

Why it matters: Surprising emotions can sometimes raise your adrenaline levels, preparing your body for a fight or flight response; this emotion has historically served to focus our attention so we can determine whether an unexpected situation presents a threat or not.

Sadness: Disappointment, grief, and sometimes hopelessness.

Why it matters: Sadness is usually our mind calling for help. It alerts us to the need to be comforted, and pulls into focus the things that matter to us most. Sadness is a crucial emotion that teaches us to adapt and grow. Without it, we would stay stuck in bad situations for longer than necessary.

Anger: A strong emotion that encompasses resentment, impatience, and frustration. It is frequently indicated by facial expressions, body language, tone of voice, and aggressive behavior.

Why it matters: We tend to regard anger as a primitive emotion that should be avoided because of its destructive power, but the purpose of anger is rooted in self-protection. It alerts us when something isn't quite right, and it begs us to examine a situation further. It could alert us to danger or unfairness.

Disgust: A protective mechanism that helps us to avoid potential threats or dangers in our environment. It is triggered by things like spoiled food, bad smells, or unsanitary conditions.

Why it matters: It's related to our survival as it helps us to avoid things that would poison us. It also has a social aspect when it is associated with moral and social judgments, like acts of cruelty or dishonesty. Understanding and recognizing our disgust response can help us to make healthier and safer choices.

Fear: a natural response to perceived threats or danger. Fear is triggered by things like a loud noise, a dark alley, or a dangerous animal.

Why it matters: It is a strong survival mechanism that helps us protect ourselves from harm. Fear is what triggers the fight or flight response, preparing us to take action to protect ourselves. Understanding and recognizing our fear response can help us reduce unnecessary fears.

learn to know your emotions

Learning to recognize and understand your emotions is the first step toward being able to control them. This involves being able to identify and label different emotions as they arise and understanding the thoughts and situations that may trigger those emotions. There are several strategies that can be helpful in learning to know your emotions:

- Pay attention to your body: Emotions often manifest physically, such as with a racing heart, a lump in your throat, or butterflies in your stomach. By paying attention to your body, you can learn to identify different emotions as they arise.

- Label your emotions: Give a name to the emotions you are feeling. It can be helpful to have a list of different emotions and their corresponding physical sensations to refer to. For example, "I feel rejected. My shoulders are tense, and my legs feel heavy".

- Reflect on your thoughts: Emotions are often linked to our thoughts. Reflecting on your thoughts and the situations that may be triggering your emotions can help you understand them better.

- Practice mindfulness: Mindfulness is the practice of being present in the moment and observing your thoughts without judging them. For instance, instead of telling yourself, "That shouldn't have made me angry," you can think, "that made me angry but I don't know why yet, and it's possible my anger is covering up a more sensitive emotion like sadness or fear." This can help you to learn to recognize your emotions as they happen. It allows you to get the benefits these strong emotions are meant to bring.

- Keep a journal: Writing down your emotions and thoughts can help you to reflect on them and understand them better. Note what triggered the emotion, how you felt, how you handled it, and what steps you took to reign it in. Refer back to it and notice how you've labeled emotions in the past and if you're learning to be more accurate in how you label your emotions.

According to many psychologists, most feelings will grow out of these six basic emotions. Learning to recognize and label your feelings and emotions properly is the first step toward taking control of them. Now that we've covered the basics let's talk about how to calm yourself down when things get intense.

5. self-regulation: how to control your emotions

. . .

 All the world is full of suffering. It is also full of overcoming.

— Helen Keller

Imagine having the power to control your emotions instead of feeling like they control you. It may sometimes feel like your emotions are all over the place, but the good news is you're not at their mercy if you improve your abilities to *self-regulate*.

Think of self-regulation as a toolbox filled with different strategies and techniques that you can use to manage your emotions. And just like with any tool, it takes time and practice to master it. But the more you work on self-regulation, the more you'll be able to navigate through life with ease and tranquility.

In earlier chapters, we talked about some ways to bring a little more peace to your mind. What about those moments when you're suddenly in the spotlight and you feel overwhelmed? Those moments when the fight/flight/freeze response is triggered.

Below we'll go over a few tactics that help you stay in control when it feels like your emotions might be taking over.

observing, not judging

An important point to recognize before moving forward is that our emotions are neither good nor bad. They're valid. They exist, they have a purpose, and they function to keep us alive, thriving, and healthy. Emotions are always there for a reason, but we don't always understand and express them properly. So when we work on controlling emotions, we aren't punishing certain ones and rewarding others; we are seeking balance.

Someone who is taught that anger is *bad* may feel ashamed for being angry and try to avoid that emotion, pushing it away and suppressing it. This isn't a great approach because anger generally tries to protect us. If we ignore this protective instinct, we might put ourselves in a bad position.

Another person who is always told, "Cheer up; things aren't that bad!" might look for ways to hide that they truly feel sad. So instead of getting to the bottom of why they feel sad, they may express anger or fake happiness to gain the approval of others.

Many people feel pressure to hide their true emotions, so I hope this chapter gives you some space to explore the things you're feeling. The more in touch you can become with your emotions, the better you'll be able to understand why you feel certain ways about things. With that understanding, big changes are possible.

cognitive reframing

This involves changing how you think about a situation in order to change how you feel about it. It may seem basic, and you would be right in thinking it is similar to some of the other exercises so far. The point of this exercise is that it can be used in the heat of the moment as things start to feel intense.

This is a simple exercise used to help reduce the intensity of negative emotions and increase positive feelings over time.

Here are the basic steps for cognitive reframing:

1. Recognize the negative thought or belief that is triggering your emotion.

2. Examine the thought:

    a. What evidence supports that thought?
    b. What evidence rejects that thought?
    c. Challenge the negative thought or belief by questioning its validity.

3. Replace the negative thought or belief with a balanced, realistic one.

4. Repeat the new positive thought or belief to yourself.

Let's use an example. Your friends are planning to go out on Friday night. You suggested a nice restaurant, but everyone shot your suggestion down. Now you're left standing there feeling a little rejected. Negative thoughts start creeping in.

Here's how we could go through this thought process using cognitive reframing:

1. **Recognize your thoughts and feelings:** *My ideas suck. These people don't even like me. No one cares about my opinion.* You may feel rejected, down, or ignored.

2. **Examine the thought:**

    a. **Evidence that supports those thoughts:** Sometimes I suggest an idea before I think about the bigger picture. That restaurant might be out of budget for some of the group.
    b. **Evidence that does not support them:** Not everyone disliked the idea; a few people agreed. My idea wasn't the only idea that the group didn't like; others got shot down too. My opinion isn't always ignored; this is just one example.

3. **Challenge the thought:** Given the evidence, are my negative thoughts valid? Is it fair to believe that all the negative thoughts and feelings in my head are true?

4. **Replace the thought:** My friends like me, and I usually feel good around them, so just because they didn't go with my idea this time doesn't mean I was rejected. Other ideas just fit the group better this time.

Can you imagine a scenario in your life where you could use this thought process to power through an intense emotion? Try to walk through this exercise using an imaginary situation. The more you practice, the more natural it should feel.

This type of thought process takes a lot of practice, and it might be difficult to get past your own negative thoughts. It's important to note that this is a widely-used practice in Cognitive Behavioral Therapy (CBT). If you struggle with this exercise or experience intense negative emotions, it would be best to work with a mental health professional. They will be able to keep things on track and guide you from a neutral perspective, making sure to address your personal needs.

self-compassion

Imagine this: being kind and understanding towards your thoughts, accepting them and appreciating them, and then letting them go. The concept of self-compassion, coined by psychologist Dr. Kristin Neff, is all about being kind and understanding towards yourself, especially during difficult times. There are three main elements:

- Self-kindness: recognizing that everyone experiences failures and hardships, so it's okay to mess up. This involves being understanding and compassionate towards yourself, letting things go, and being as kind to yourself as you would to a friend or loved one.

- Common humanity: seeing your own struggles from a wider perspective, recognizing that challenging moments are part of being human. This element recognizes that we are part of a bigger picture. We all struggle, and we are surrounded by people who can relate to our struggles. Life is challenging at times, and this gives it meaning.

- Mindfulness: taking a balanced approach to negative emotions by observing them with openness. You don't get overly caught up in negative thoughts or feelings, and they are no more or less important than other emotions. This allows us to be present in the current moment and accept things instead of avoiding them.

Self-compassion isn't about pretending everything is totally fine and perfect; it recognizes that life is messy and complicated, but that there is a lot to enjoy even though we all suffer to some degree.

What does this concept have to do with social anxiety? Because anxiety frequently overwhelms our thoughts with negative self-talk. Practicing self-compassion gives your mind a platform to approach your thoughts and inner dialogue from a place of kindness. It does not push criticism and judgment away; it just puts those thoughts into perspective.

When doing any of the exercises in this book, try to keep the concepts of self-compassion in mind. Here are a few tips to make that easier:

- Notice when you are being self-critical and try to reframe your thoughts in a compassionate way. For example, instead of thinking, "I'm an idiot; I can't do anything right," try to approach it from 3 different angles:

    ° Self-kindness: *I made a mistake, but that doesn't make me an idiot.*
    ° Common humanity: *We all make mistakes and that's actually the best way to learn some things.*
    ° Mindfulness: *What are the impacts of that mistake? What did I learn, and where do I go from here?*

- Practice self-care activities that nourish your body, mind, and spirit, such as exercising, getting enough sleep, eating a healthy diet, and engaging in activities that bring you joy.

• Try using affirmations and self-compassionate phrases to remind yourself that you are worthy of care and respect. Some examples include "I am worthy of love and respect," "I am doing the best that I can," and "It's okay to make mistakes."

By testing your thoughts and approaching them with self-compassion, it is possible to cultivate a healthier and more positive inner dialogue.

In conclusion, emotional regulation is important for overall well-being and mental health. It can empower you to manage your emotions in a healthy way rather than becoming overwhelmed by them or acting impulsively. It can also help you to build and maintain healthy relationships, giving you the power to express your emotions in a constructive way.

key takeaways

- Emotional regulation is the ability to manage and control your emotions in a healthy and adaptive way.
- We all have highs and lows, but there are ways to control our emotional output
- Use Cognitive Reframing to challenge negative thoughts
- Self-compassion is the emotionally healthy mindset of accepting yourself without judgment, acknowledging the good *and* the bad, and staying present in the moment

6. building confidence

. . .

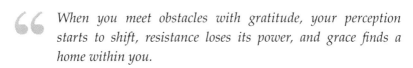 *When you meet obstacles with gratitude, your perception starts to shift, resistance loses its power, and grace finds a home within you.*

— Oprah Winfrey

At the root of many peoples' social anxiety lies constant negative self-talk and a lack of self-confidence. So, we will get into some strategies that work on building an emotionally healthy relationship with yourself.

goal setting

One great way to build your confidence is to set small, achievable goals for yourself. These could be related to school, sports, getting better at a hobby, or any personal development goal you can think of. Make sure to celebrate your success, which could mean telling others what you achieved, treating yourself, and reminding yourself of your strengths and accomplishments.

practice social skills in different settings

Interacting with others can be intimidating, especially if you haven't had much practice. Would you feel comfortable joining a team or club at your school? Have you thought about joining a group activity in your community or in a different town nearby instead? Sometimes it's really helpful to break into a different group of people. They don't know you yet, so you've got a chance to start fresh. Maybe you're interested in things that aren't offered nearby, so it could help to branch out a little.

write aimlessly in a journal

Writing down your thoughts and feelings can be a helpful way to process and manage everything going on in your life. Try writing for a few minutes each day, focusing on your negative thoughts and how you can reframe them in a more positive way. For example, you could write down a negative thought, such as "I thought I wasn't good enough, but then…" and then come up with a more interesting thought. It's your private space to write, so you can even get unrealistic. Make up a fantasy, play with unrealistic ideas, and make it fun. You can get a nice notebook and write on paper if you like, or type this out - it doesn't make a difference as long as you're expressing yourself and letting your thoughts run free.

As an adult, I use a journal every single day to write down all the thoughts in my head right after I wake up. It's amazing to see how many disconnected thoughts swirl around my brain from the minute I open my eyes in the morning. By writing, I sometimes learn that something is taking up a lot of space in my head that I hadn't even realized. My journal entries don't tell a story and they don't always make sense. They just give me space to clear all the things out of my mind and put my thoughts onto paper. It helps to quiet my anxious inner voice and allows me to focus on the day ahead.

seek out positive influences

Surrounding yourself with positive people, like friends and family members who are supportive and uplifting, can help to reduce negative self-talk. All of us have role models and people we admire.

Think about who you look up to and what is so positive about their example. Negativity comes at us from every direction, all day, every day. Focusing on people doing great things can be inspiring, and it helps to push yourself toward that kind of accomplishment.

think positive

If you catch yourself thinking negatively, change your focus. Instead of replaying what went wrong, consider what you will do differently next time and what you have learned.

Positive affirmations work really well for some people. It could be helpful to fill the void during quiet moments with positive affirmations instead of allowing your mind to wander, especially if it wanders to negative places.

It might feel really uncomfortable at first, but some research shows that you don't even need to believe the affirmations for them to have a positive impact. Some examples of positive affirmations are:

- I am loved
- My uniqueness is my superpower
- I don't need to compare myself to anyone else
- I believe in my abilities
- My talents will take me far in life
- I'm valuable
- My charisma is unstoppable
- I deserve to take up space here
- I am in control of my life
- I am not influenced by the opinions of others

Affirmations work better for some people than others, but the point is it never hurts to add a little positivity to the quiet moments, especially if your mind sometimes wanders to dark places.

live in the moment

Your inner dialogue frequently revolves around the past ('what could have been') and the future ('what could be'). The only time you can actually make a change is in the present. The past and future are fantasy, so you've got a way better chance at making a real difference if you just focus on the present.

Being present quiets your internal debate and allows you to concentrate on and enjoy what is happening around you.

practice gratitude

Your brain is not necessarily built to seek out positivity and appreciation. It is a problem-solving machine, and it got extremely good at that over the course of human existence.

This is a blessing and a curse because our brains might see a good situation and, instead of thinking, "Woah, this is amazing!" it will wonder how to make it even better. On the other hand, when presented with a bad situation, our brains will focus on fixing it - and when our mind is focused on making a negative situation better, it's hard to notice the positive.

A ton of studies have proven that people who show kindness, give thanks to others, and focus their minds on expressing gratitude, live healthier and happier lives. When we do something nice for someone else, chemicals in our brains reward us with a boost of good energy.

Here are a few simple ways to keep gratitude a priority in your life:

• Keep a gratitude journal where you write down a few things you are grateful for each day

  ° They can be tiny things, like your friend complimenting your outfit, having time to treat yourself to a snack before school, or even a small favor from someone at school.

° Reflect: How did those things make you feel? What values of yours did they reward? Why are you thankful for them?

• Consider ways to express gratitude for those things, such as writing a thank-you note or performing a small act of kindness

° It doesn't have to be big, but if someone has made you feel good, think about some way to return that feeling back to them.
° You can even write a note you don't plan on giving to someone. Just the act of writing down some heartfelt, kind words can make you feel great.

• Verbalize your gratitude to someone you appreciate and explain why you are grateful for that person

° This could be as simple as telling a classmate you appreciate their help with a homework assignment.

• Participate in volunteer work in your community

° Volunteering is a great way to widen your perspective and see all the different lives of the people who live around us.
° When you put effort into a cause that interests you, it becomes easier to connect with others who have similar interests

• Reflect on the positive impact these activities have on your own well-being and the well-being of others.

° Allow yourself to feel good about any of these activities.
° Don't belittle them, and recognize that you have done something positive for yourself and the world around you

key takeaways

- Self-confidence is an important part of relieving symptoms of social anxiety
- By focusing on positive influences and getting in touch with our thoughts we can improve the way we view ourselves
- Practicing gratitude is a proven way to improve self-confidence by making a positive impact on the world around you and focusing on the good things.

7. be the master of your inner dialogue

. . .

> Worry often gives a small thing a big shadow.
>
> — Swedish proverb

We've talked a little bit about negative self-talk in the previous chapters, but now let's dive deeper and show you how to take control of that inner voice.

Your inner dialogue has a massive influence on your opinion of yourself, so it's crucial to get in touch with it and learn the power you have to control it. This chapter will discuss the role of thoughts and beliefs in shaping our identity and how to challenge and reframe negative thoughts.

Ultimately, you will have a better understanding of how to control your inner dialogue and manage strong emotions.

Pay close attention to the negative thoughts that come up as you read through this chapter. As you get closer to realizing how useless that negativity is, your negative inner voice might start chattering even louder.

getting in touch with your inner voice

Think about the thoughts that swirl around your head throughout the day. Can you remember any specific things you tell yourself? Is there a certain tone your inner voice has? What kind of moments does your inner saboteur begin screaming the loudest? In what kind of situations does your inner cheerleader encourage you the strongest?

Your inner dialogue is sneaky because it is barely noticeable, yet it's always working overtime. The thoughts it repeatedly sends through your mind eventually become beliefs. As we start to believe something and accept it as truth, we begin to identify with it.

So if you constantly tell yourself you don't have what it takes to succeed at something, that thought is going to grow legs and start running through your mind. If you fail to challenge that thought, or you don't even notice it's there, you might begin to accept this anti-success story as your truth without any proof. Once that sets in, it is natural to identify as a person who just doesn't have what it takes to succeed. That's messed up! It's not valid because it's based on nothing but negative imaginary thoughts.

Our inner dialogue is part of what makes us human. It questions bad decisions and tries to keep us away from risky situations, like the feeling you get when you are too close to the edge of a cliff.

Sometimes anxiety can take over and warn us about something that is not actually risky, like what happens when we need to speak in front of a large crowd. Public speaking is scary, but it's not physically danger-ous. When someone is prone to anxiety, their thoughts can amplify the negative inner voice that would normally be trying to keep them safe. Then, it works in a vicious cycle that intensifies the negative thoughts until they've grown out of proportion and we truly believe them.

Your thoughts have a huge impact on your mood, self-confidence, and self-esteem, so the voice in your head has a good side and a bad side. When the inner dialogue is under control and positive thoughts are the norm, everything feels better. The positive thoughts will reinforce more positive thoughts and see the bright side of anything negative that comes along. Unfortunately, the same goes with negative thoughts - they will push away positivity and keep spinning around, getting more and more negative. Here are some strategies to help you manage your inner dialogue.

recognizing your inner dialogue

You must first become more aware of what your internal dialogue is telling you. The thoughts and ideas it repeats all day, every day, are mostly ignored, so even if you are pretty in tune with it, you might be surprised when you begin to listen closely to what that voice is saying.

recognizing complex emotions

Do you ever struggle to figure out exactly how you feel? Is it ever hard to express your thoughts and feelings clearly because there are so many things swirling around your head? Well, what a lot of people are surprised to learn is that many of the emotions we feel are actually feelings about *other emotions*, not feelings about things that have happened.

Let's break that down a little. Let's say you've got a classmate named Daniel. Your teacher hands his test back to him and he got a really bad grade. The very first thing he feels is disappointment. He is disappointed in himself because he knows he didn't study enough. He could have done better but he was lazy and didn't prepare, so he's disappointed and a little ashamed. Feeling this way is deep; it's a raw emotion.

Feeling this raw emotion makes Daniel feel sensitive and vulnerable, and no one wants to stay in that mental place for long. So next, he gets angry. It feels less vulnerable to be angry than disappointed in himself. Let's say he directed his anger outward and slammed his fist onto his desk, and yelled something about the test being unfair.

In this example, Daniel felt disappointed as a reaction to the bad grade. That was his *primary emotion*; it was raw and personal, and it was his brain's first instinctive reaction. But then, anger took over as a response to feeling disappointed in himself. Anger is the *secondary emotion* because it was his reaction to feeling disappointed once his brain had a chance to process the primary emotion and the situation. His anger was a way to protect himself from sensitivity and vulnerability.

Maybe it didn't stop there. Once Daniel made a scene in class, he might feel embarrassed because of how he expressed his anger. Since embarrassment is another sensitive emotion, he might become sad or even go back to anger again. He could go through several more emotions, each one a reaction to the previous emotion. All of these feelings stemmed from one event (getting a bad grade) but then spiraled out of control in a chain reaction.

By the end of it, Daniel would probably have a really hard time explaining how he even feels or why he's in that emotional state. The chain reaction of emotions makes it hard to identify where any of them came from.

Anger is a common secondary emotion, and a lot of times, people have trouble figuring out exactly where it came from. This is part of the reason anger is looked down upon. On its own, anger is a pure, protective emotion. But when it's allowed to take over as a protective secondary emotion, its defensive characteristics can produce pretty toxic results.

Do you know why we get defensive when someone strikes a nerve? This same process is typically how defensiveness takes hold. Imagine a friend calls you selfish. How does that play out in your head and in your actions? Your primary emotion may feel sad, guilty, or insecure, wondering if you might be selfish sometimes. It's easy for anger to take over here, though, because it's more comfortable to be angry in response to a hurtful comment than to examine it and talk about the sensitive feelings that come along.

Embracing primary emotions and connecting with others

Being able to understand and manage your emotions is a powerful tool. You can't always believe everything your emotions tell you to feel. But instead of avoiding or ignoring intense feelings, try to explore them and see what they're trying to teach you.

Any time you feel an intense emotion, it is worth questioning the source. Primary emotions help us connect better to others, while secondary emotions push people away. All of our emotions are equally valid, so it's no good if your secondary emotions are allowed to take over and make you forget the primary ones.

It's easier to connect with people when you deal with your primary emotions since they give a better idea of who you are and what you value. Secondary emotions do none of that. They build a wall between you and your primary emotions, making it harder to understand yourself, which makes it harder to connect with others.

It's important to know what thoughts and feelings make you feel vulnerable. These are the ones most likely to trigger secondary emotions that can get in the way. Like everything else, this will take some practice, but if you keep a curious mindset when it comes to your emotions, you will be prepared.

Here are a few steps to recognize your instinctual primary emotions:

- Take a few deep breaths to calm your body and clear your mind
- Think about what you're feeling. Where do you feel it in your body, and what physical effects does this emotion have? What word or words would you use to describe what you're feeling?
- Ask yourself, "where is this feeling coming from?" Remember to stay curious - you are just considering possibilities
- Go back to the first moment you remember noticing these intense feelings. What sparked the intensity? Try to think of the exact thing that happened.
- Finally, ask yourself if the initial spark that caused this intense reaction might have confronted something you're sensitive about or protective of. Is there an emotion that makes you feel vulnerable beneath all of this?

Event: Got a Bad Grade

Your teacher hands back a test and it's a bad grade.
You know you didn't prepare well, and you let yourself and others down.
You a little surprised and you feel disappointed

Primary Emotion: Disappointed

Feeling this way isn't cool. It's vulnerable and your mind is already making moves to feel less of this.

Angry is an easier emotion to express. You begin to feel anger sink in.

Secondary Emotion: Angry

This secondary emotion helps to push away the unpleasant primary emotion.

In this situation, anger is protective and avoidant because it is covering up your instinctual reaction.

Managing Emotion

When emotions pile on top of each other, it gets difficult to identify them.

When we try to hide our natural feelings (disappointment in this example) we cause ourselves extra stress and fall out of touch with ourselves.

It can be helpful to practice recognizing your emotions in a calm setting, like after the fact in writing. Grab your journal and let your thoughts flow out. This can help you identify what you're really feeling instead of just reacting to surface-level emotions.

By learning to manage your emotions, you'll have better relationships, be happier, and have more control over your life. So, the next time you're feeling overwhelmed, try exploring your emotions and seeing what they have to teach you.

These concepts are getting advanced and that might have been intense. How is your inner dialogue? Are the negative voices speaking up louder than usual at this point? I mentioned this at the start of the chapter, but our inner saboteur tends to get more aggressive as we get closer to taking back some of its power.

Be prepared for your inner voice to insult you and make you feel embarrassed for confronting its negativity. It might insist all of this is pointless because it doesn't want you to grow out of it. That was my experience when I started all of this, anyway. But I cringed through it. By keeping up the work, I realized how badly my inner dialogue wanted to hold me back from growing out of the negative thought patterns that were keeping me small.

key takeaways

- Your inner dialogue is always at work, so learn to pay attention to what it's saying to you
- All emotions are valid, and they have a purpose in trying to teach us something
- Mindfulness meditation is one of the best ways to get in touch and make peace with your inner dialogue
- Many of the emotions we experience are a reaction to other emotions, making them hard to express or explain
- Sometimes certain emotions take over, causing an imbalance in our thought processes and emotional responses

- Intense emotions usually come from a triggering event, and they can cause a chain reaction of emotional responses that can be overwhelming
- Stay curious when you feel intense emotions. Explore them and learn where they are coming from
- Embracing the primary emotions that make us feel vulnerable is a super power that allows us to build stronger bonds with others, as well as get to know ourselves

8. prepare for exposure to triggers

. . .

 He who sweats more in training bleeds less in war.

— Greek Proverb

Dealing with triggers can be intense and this content could be emotionally challenging for some. When faced with triggers that cause distress, seek to work through them with a mental health professional.

Anxiety triggers are things that make your brain think something is dangerous, even if it is not. This can cause physical symptoms like muscle tension, stomach problems, and trouble breathing. Since these symptoms are so uncomfortable, you might avoid certain things or situations altogether.

For example, if you have social anxiety, you might avoid hanging out with friends, attending after-school events, or even going to the store. But the good news is that you can take some simple steps to make your anxiety triggers less overwhelming.

The first step is to figure out what they are, so you can be prepared. Here are some of the most common things that can trigger anxiety:

- **Public speaking or giving a presentation:** Speaking in front of a group of people can cause a lot of anxiety since it involves being the center of attention. Just the thought of that can activate the body's fight or flight response, leading to symptoms such as increased heart rate, sweating, and difficulty speaking. Additionally, people may fear being judged harshly or rejected by the audience.

- **Meeting new people or going to parties:** Nothing induces social anxiety more than a room full of strangers. Meeting new people or attending a party where you don't know anyone can be difficult. It may increase your concern if someone you find attractive, or someone you look up to is going to be there.

- **Dating:** Dating can be awkward for everyone, but for some socially anxious people, it can be downright overwhelming. Many elements of dating can cause anxiety, from initiating phone calls to going on first dates, or just speaking to someone you find attractive.

- **Reading out loud:** Some people are afraid to read in public. This anxiety has a lot to do with being the center of attention. Reading aloud in front of others can trigger the same feelings of fear as public speaking and can cause the same physical symptoms like shakiness and sweating. The same thing can happen if you need to write or type as other people watch.

- **Expressing your thoughts when you disagree:** Do you avoid expressing your point of view? Do you accept what others say even if you disagree? Some people are frightened to express their ideas for fear of being judged, so they have trouble setting boundaries and standing up for what they know is right.

- **Eating in public:** Some people are afraid of eating in public. They may be terrified of spilling a drink or eating in front of people in positions of authority, or they may be concerned that others will harshly judge the way they eat.

identifying and managing your specific triggers

Do you relate to any of those triggers? Are there other things that trigger anxiety for you that weren't listed?

Think about the situations you find most difficult. How does your body react? What thoughts run through your mind? Do you normally avoid those situations completely or have you already found some ways to cope?

Knowing the situations that cause you the most anxiety is the first step in developing healthy coping techniques. By identifying triggers, you can learn to recognize the early signs of anxiety and take steps to prevent it from escalating.

practice relaxation techniques

Before you go into a situation that causes anxiety, try some relaxation techniques to start off on a calm note. In chapter 3, we covered deep breathing and progressive muscle relaxation. We challenged thoughts in chapter 5 and talked about mindfulness meditation in chapter 6. Have you practiced any of those yet?

A lot of times, we get nervous and worried when our mind has nothing else to distract it. If you find yourself getting worried in a quiet moment, use one (or all) of these exercises to get your mind back to center.

set small goals

Rather than trying to tackle all things at once, set small goals for yourself. This might include starting a conversation with one person, joining a small group activity, or getting more comfortable making eye contact with others.

focus on the present moment

When socializing with peers, try to stay present in the moment and avoid getting caught up in negative thoughts about the future or the past. Also, avoid letting your mind wander or getting caught up in thoughts about what anyone might be thinking. Stick to what's happening in front of you.

It's really difficult to be a good active listener when we're not present in the moment. If you're zoning out of a conversation, it's easy to lose track of what's going on and say something unrelated to what the group is talking about.

notice *limiting beliefs* and replace them with *empowering beliefs*

Your inner dialogue is usually extra active when you're getting ready to go into a triggering situation. Be ready for negativity, and don't let it get away with reinforcing limiting beliefs!

Some negative thoughts to watch out for:

- I don't have what it takes to do this well
- If this isn't great, no one will ever take me seriously
- I'll trip over my words
- This is too hard
- People will think I'm dumb

And then some positive, empowering beliefs to counter them with:

- I have what it takes to succeed at this and at anything else I put an effort into
- I'll do great at this and I'll keep improving every time I try again
- I'll speak clearly and confidently
- I am capable of doing difficult things
- People like me and they'll appreciate my efforts

- I am in control of my life
- I'm in control of myself in this moment

take a break.

Anxiety can make us see a mountain out of an ant hill. When you're overcome with fear or worry, it's tough to think clearly. The first step is to take some time to calm down physically. When it gets intense, give yourself a breather. Take a few minutes and go walk around the block, grab a drink or a snack, chat with a friend - anything that keeps you active and removes you from the situation for a few minutes.

breathe through the fear.

If you notice a quicker heartbeat or sweaty palms, it is better not to resist it. Stay where you are and try not to distract yourself from the panic. Notice that it's starting, but remember you are entirely in control. Did you try the deep breathing exercise in Chapter 3? This would be the same.

don't strive for perfection.

We are bombarded by images of beautiful people with tons of money living perfect lives all day, every day. Bad days and disappointments are inevitable, and real life is not all that we see on social media. By practicing gratitude, you gain respect for where you are in your journey of life, and it becomes less important to compare yourself to others (or the images they portray of their lives).

consider a joyful place.

Close your eyes for a moment and visualize a haven of safety and peace. Maybe you're on the beach or curled up in bed with your cat next to you, or it's a joyful childhood memory of you running around having fun. Allow the pleasant feelings to calm you down until you feel more at ease.

don't be your own worst critic

It's normal to feel anxious when socializing and remember that it's fine to make mistakes or feel awkward. Be kind to yourself and try to focus on the progress you are making rather than any setbacks.

In conclusion, understanding and identifying your anxiety triggers is a big step in managing your anxiety. By recognizing what causes your symptoms, you can develop strategies to cope with those triggers and take steps to prevent them from escalating. Whether it's public speaking, social interactions, or even mundane tasks, everyone's experience with anxiety is unique, and it's important to approach it in a non-judgmental way.

By learning simple coping techniques, you can take control and improve your overall well-being. Remember, it's important to be patient with yourself and to know that managing anxiety takes time and practice. Small steps are always better than no steps! Any small step you take today will have a massive impact as you keep learning and improving.

key takeaways

- Preparing for exposure to triggers can be stressful, so it's important to know what situations you struggle with the most.
- If you're nervous about something in the future, work on relaxation techniques to help you reframe the situation and feel calmer.
- Try out as many healthy coping skills as often as possible and find what works for you.

9. find your people

. . .

 Haters are like crickets. You can hear all the noise they make, but you can't see them… Then, right when you walk by them, they're quiet.

— Dean Bokhari

A sense of belonging is important to all of us as humans because it provides a sense of security. Belonging to a group was crucial to our survival back when we were hunter-gatherers. While we don't need to band together to avoid death by saber-tooth tiger anymore, feeling connected and valued by others remains crucial to our happiness.

For teenagers, a sense of belonging is especially important. At this point in your life, you are in the process of developing your own identity and forming relationships that matter to you. It's pretty common for teens to put an unhealthy amount of pressure on themselves to win approval.

Belonging to a positive and supportive group of friends can provide you with a sense of direction and set you on the right path. In this chapter, you will explore how to find the people and activities that bring you joy. We'll talk about some options you may not have already thought of, and you'll do some exercises that get you thinking outside the box.

Not everything is going to work for you - and that's how it should be! The important thing is to expose yourself to new activities, potentially interesting situations, and challenges that entertain you, build your confidence and let you grow.

The best thing you can do during your teenage years – actually, well into your 20s – is to try things, fail at them, learn from those failures, and grow into a person who is very certain of what is worth your time.

Our society is obsessed with success, but this isn't productive. Look into any famous person you can think of, and I guarantee you their path to the top was filled with failure, self-doubt, and all kinds of obstacles. Most successful people had haters trying to bring them down the entire time they were fighting their way to the top. So, instead of focusing on succeeding, focus on a goal and prepare to fail many times on your way to finally reaching it.

As you set on your path to try new things, meet new people, and join different groups, be prepared for it to feel awkward and unnatural at first. Give everything a chance and know that no decision you make is permanent.

Let's dive into a few ways to focus on things that bring you joy and find groups that you would want to belong to.

embrace your uniqueness!

A lot of people fall into the trap of pushing their unique qualities away to focus on things that help them fit into a larger group. With over 8 billion of us on the planet, there are literally millions of different hobbies, topics, activities, and interests people are bonding over.

Let's take a second to get in touch with what you already know you're interested in, and then let's jog your mind to see if there are other things you might tap into. Grab a piece of paper, doodle on a tablet, or get artistic if that's your thing. The point is to let your mind wander all over the place, leaving any limiting beliefs behind.

- Start by listing the interests or hobbies that you already have. These could be things you enjoy doing in your free time, such as reading, playing sports, or listening to music.

- Next, create another list with things you've always wanted to try but haven't yet. These could be things you've heard about or seen others doing that you're curious about, such as painting, dancing, or rock climbing.

- Now make a list of all the things you loved when you were a kid. What are some childhood activities, toys, or games that you really loved? List a few things that bring a smile to your face.

- For the next list, imagine that money is not an object. What would you start doing if you had an infinite amount of money at your disposal? Build a skyscraper? Reincarnate dinosaurs? Study wildlife in a far-away place?

- Location is not a limiting factor for this final list. You can stay in your hometown or be all the way across the world. You have complete freedom of movement, and you don't have to stay anywhere for a long time. What would you do? What languages are spoken, and what music do you hear playing? What's the food like? Are you hanging out in cities, on the beach, or in the mountains?

Now look back at the lists you've made. What patterns can you identify? Does the music you listen to at home originate from another country you'd visit if you could, for example? Do your interests revolve around craving new experiences or staying rooted close to home? Does being alone give you more energy than group activities?

Are there certain cultures, topics, sports, or hobbies that exist on multiple lists?

Find as many patterns as you can. By giving your brain room to be imaginative during the exercise, you allowed your inner dialogue to tell you something you may not have known about yourself. These patterns didn't just come out of nowhere - they came from your inner voice communicating subconsciously.

Earlier, we discussed how your inner dialogue has both a good side and a bad side. This exercise allowed you to tap into its good side. Now that you've given your brain a chance to think outside the box let's talk about getting out of your comfort zone.

get out of your comfort zone *one step at a time*

- Once you have a list of interests, start researching groups or organizations in your community that align with them. Look for clubs, teams, classes, or online spaces that are related to these interests.

- Look for volunteer opportunities, too.

- As you research, make a list of the different groups or organizations you find. Include the name of the group, a brief description, and what you like about it so far.

- Think about one or two groups or organizations you would like to explore further. Check it out online or, even better, ask someone who is already involved to learn more about their activities and how to join.

- Sign yourself up!

It's okay to try different groups or activities before finding the right fit. Give everything a try. Keep an open mind. It would be a shame to quit something because you're intimidated, because you're not good at it yet, or because you haven't gotten to know the group well enough. My parents never let me quit anything when I was a kid, but guess what - I grew into a huge fan of quitting. But I'll only quit once I *know* something isn't for me.

Let's say you've gone out on a limb with something new and given it a few tries. You haven't learned anything that excites you, it doesn't give you energy, and you don't see any future in it. No one in the group seems interesting to you, and you've tried to connect with some of the group members, but you haven't gotten anywhere with it. If that's really true, quit it! Move on to the next thing. You can always come back to it later if you have regrets.

I was forced to join a soccer team when I was 8 years old. I hated it, I wasn't good at it, none of my teammates became friends, and I never improved. Soccer just wasn't for me. My grandma actually *still* laughs at how I just sort of spun around on the field, as far away from the action as I could be. I would have rather been at home building Legos by myself instead of embarrassing myself on a field in front of all the athletic kids and their parents.

But it was honestly an experience that taught me a lot. I learned what it felt like to stick to something I was awful at. I was forced into a social circle I had nothing in common with. I learned how to completely detach myself from the task at hand because it left me joyless. I would have quit, but that experience didn't cause me distress, and my parents knew it was good for me to suffer a little in that way.

On the other hand, I joined a band in high school that I thought was so cool. I loved their music and idolized the band members. A few weeks in, though, I realized they all secretly hated each other. It was a toxic environment that ruined my whole image of them. I still wanted to be involved with this band and the attention that came with it, but their vibe was dragging me down. We practiced together for a few weeks, and I even started connecting with some of them. Still, I couldn't trust that any of them actually liked me with all the backstabbing I was witnessing.

So, I quit. We stayed on good terms and said *hi* when we saw each other, but I was so happy to be out of a situation I had started to dread. I went back and forth in my mind wondering if I had made the right choice, because I did miss the coolness of being in the band. But when I thought back about how it made me feel, I knew it wasn't for me. They even asked me a few months later if I would think about joining again. So, I had options.

Nothing is forever, so if you try something you end up disliking, you can just quit and try something new after you've given it a chance. If you've quit something prematurely, you can always go back to it. The best thing you can do for yourself is to get out of your comfort zone.

look for other people that do what you love to do

The good news is that it's easier than ever to connect with others who share your passions. Whether it's knitting animal hats, collecting rocks, listening to obscure folk music, or reading poetry in another language, you're bound to find a group of people dedicated to the subject online.

Just search for groups or communities related to your hobbies and join them. Introduce yourself, and don't be afraid to admit that you're completely new to something. People usually love teaching something they are interested in, and people are generally helpful.

Keep in mind that it may take some time to find your tribe. You might have to explore different groups and interests before finding the right fit. But when you find a group of people who "get" you, don't be afraid to jump in and get involved.

don't be afraid to let people go

If you've read this far, you are clearly committed to your personal growth, overcoming challenges, and getting the most out of life. That's a tough journey and it may feel lonely at times, especially if you're not getting the support you would expect from people around you. The fact is, it's scary to break out of your comfort zone, and not everyone will be cheering you along. Some may even make fun of you for trying to change, belittle your efforts, or try to make you feel like you're abandoning them.

Want to surround yourself with people who make you happy and have your best interest at heart? It's okay to walk away from people who don't. No need to be rude, but you don't have to spend time with people who tear you down or hold you back.

That's not to say you're superior for prioritizing growth or that they are inferior for being satisfied where they are. Everyone moves at a different pace, and it's important to respect where everyone is in their life. But it is crucial to expose yourself to people who encourage you, challenge you to overcome obstacles, and inspire you.

look for those who are on similar paths

Having a diverse group of people in your life is important, and it's valuable to interact with individuals from various backgrounds and experiences. I grew up in a part of New York City where most of the people in my neighborhood came from different countries and cultural backgrounds. Looking back, I realize we all learned a lot from each other thanks to our differences.

Your friend group doesn't need to be built around people with all the same interests or background as you, but it's important to be friends with people who are on the same path, with similar values, and with the same general goals in life.

It's helpful to be around people who may be ahead of you in some ways, whether they're a year older, better at a sport, more advanced in a class, or a skill you'd like to master. They can show you the way and inspire you when you doubt yourself.

Not everyone will understand your journey. Having just a few close friends who support you and your goals is okay.

look for quality over quantity

The best friend goals focus on the quality of relationships rather than the quantity. Having a small group of close friends who truly understand and support you is much more valuable than having a large circle of people you don't feel like yourself around. Your close friends should be people you can trust, confide in, and rely on.

They should also be people who you can learn from, grow with, and have fun with. Ultimately, the goal should be to surround yourself with people who bring out the best in you and make you feel good about yourself.

master showing empathy

Connecting with new people is a superpower, and people naturally gravitate toward people who make them feel good. Being empathetic and kind can make you someone everyone wants to be around. They will feel comfortable sharing things with you, which will help you form a deeper bond over time.

Empathy is sometimes described as putting yourself in someone else's shoes, but in reality, it goes deeper than that. People have different lived experiences depending on superficial qualities like skin color, religion, socio-economic status, and the list goes on. We all perceive events differently based on our past, how our mind interprets things, where we grew up, and a number of other factors.

By being truly empathetic, we acknowledge that we don't completely understand someone else. Did you happen to do the empathy card exercise in chapter 2? That exercise is great at showing how each of us experiences and acts out the same event in a very different way.

How would you feel if you were going through a breakup? How would you want to be treated? Now, imagine one of your friends treating you the opposite way. Let's say you want to be left alone and quietly process your thoughts about what happened. They, on the other hand, are the type that would want to talk this out and go over every possible scenario. So, they put themselves in your shoes. They ask a ton of questions and propose reasons why the breakup happened. They won't leave it alone and it makes you even more upset. They have imagined how *they* would want to be treated and done the same to you. We all do this sometimes, so it's not a bad thing, but it's not always such a compassionate thing.

Empathy would be that friend taking the time to understand how you deal with this kind of situation and what you would need to feel better. Once they have learned what works for you, they would try to deliver on that.

key takeaways

- Belonging to a positive and supportive group of friends is essential
- In finding your people, look for quality over quantity.
- It's easier to find the right people when you know what you want. Exercises to get in touch with your interests are a great place to start.
- Showing empathy is the purest way to form deeper connections between people

10. the right mindset

. . .

> *The future rewards those who press on. I don't have time to feel sorry for myself. I don't have time to complain. I'm going to press on.*

— Barack Obama

In the previous chapters, we have explored a few ways to build confidence, overcome negative thoughts, cope with negative emotions, and find your passion.

Maybe you have worked on some of the exercises, maybe not yet. But now is the time to act!

We can talk about anxiety all day, but nothing changes until we begin exposing ourselves, little by little, to the things that cause angst.

Without exposure, anxiety gets worse. That little voice in your head gets stronger, and your thoughts become beliefs, which eventually turn into something you identify with. But now you know a few ways to make your life easier.

It's not comfortable when you begin to confront your fears and take control of your life. So, this chapter is a quick pep talk and a couple of reminders to help you maintain a strong mindset that will tackle anything standing in your way.

remember: don't give in to avoidance

We covered how avoiding social situations may seem like an easy way to reduce anxiety, but it can actually make everything worse in the long run. Avoidance reinforces the thoughts telling you that social situations are dangerous, so your mind believes it is necessary to avoid them in order to keep you safe. This can result in a cycle of avoidance, increased anxiety, and eventually identifying as someone who is simply unable to do certain things.

On the other hand, engaging in social situations, especially when it feels uncomfortable or anxiety-provoking at first, will help to challenge and gradually reduce the fear of social situations.

It can also help to build confidence and improve social skills. It's important to remember that social anxiety is extremely common and it's treatable. It is possible to learn new skills and feel more confident in social situations with practice and support.

Starting with small steps and gradually exposing yourself to more challenging social situations over time is the best way to go. It can also be helpful to seek the assistance of a mental health professional who can provide support and guidance in overcoming social anxiety.

gradually expose yourself to social situations

Take small steps. Each of us has different strengths, and we're all struggling in different areas. If speaking up in class is hard for you, pick a moment to participate in a conversation about something you're interested in and just dive in headfirst. If you spend a lot of time alone and don't know where to start socializing, engage with a group online that discusses something you're into.

Don't try to take it on all at once and allow yourself to enjoy the process. You'll get a huge rush of dopamine (the brain chemical that makes you happy) when you conquer a fear. Sit with that rush of joy and let it be the incentive to conquer an even bigger fear.

A friend of mine is a personal trainer. She tells me that most people will join a gym with the best intentions, work out a few times and never go again. They strain their muscles, they don't have fun, and they don't want to continue putting time and effort into an unfamiliar routine. They never become comfortable going to the gym. They think they don't belong, which turns into the belief they don't belong there. Then *poof!* they're gone, never to be seen in that gym again.

So she uses a unique strategy to keep her new clients motivated. I like this because even though the example is for a workout routine, the tactic itself can be applied to making any kind of habit.

Here's what she advises:

- Week 1, go to the gym 2 times for 20 minutes each. You won't feel like you did much at all, but you've exposed yourself to the gym and you haven't worked too hard or pulled any muscles. You're just warming up to the idea of actually being in that space.

- Week 2, go to the gym 3 times for 20 minutes each. You'll get more done, but you're still not stressing your body out, and you're not suddenly dedicating a ton of time to the new routine. You get a chance to ease into the habit, and you're even more comfortable inside the walls of the gym.

- Week 3, go to the gym 4 times for 30 minutes each. Same idea, just adding one more visit and ten extra minutes. Doing anything four days a week is a lot, but it's just a 30-minute session so it doesn't take too much time away from the day. This allows the habit to start forming.

- Week 4, they implement the normal schedule according to the client's workout goals.

If you've got a gym goal, go ahead and use that free advice from my trainer friend! But this applies to any habit you'd like to form. Start small so the first few times almost feel too easy and leave you wanting more. Gradually increase how demanding the situation is so you can grow and improve. Eventually, you'll be in the habit of doing this new thing and it will be easier to continue.

Reward yourself for taking even the tiniest steps. Push out any negative thoughts or limiting beliefs that try to steal the joy away from that accomplishment. It doesn't matter where anyone else is in their journey, and it doesn't matter where anyone thinks you should be.

This is all about you. If you want to make improvements, work on your own schedule and do all you can do. Anything that moves you forward is worth celebrating. Take a second to think about an area for improvement you'd like to work on. Can you see yourself gradually introducing this new thing to your life, using the above strategy?

build communication skills and boost your self-confidence - it's a loop

Effective communication is a critical skill for building and maintaining relationships with others. When we are able to communicate effectively, we are more likely to feel confident and capable in social situations, which can improve our overall social skills. Here are some specific strategies for building communication skills:

- **Practice active listening**

This involves paying attention to the speaker, asking clarifying questions, and providing feedback to show that you are understanding and engaged in the conversation. Active listening can help to build trust and improve interpersonal relationships.

- **Celebrate your differences**

Instead of trying to fit in or hide your differences, celebrate them. Embracing what makes you unique can help you stand out and feel confident in your own skin.

- **Use your strengths in social situations**

Consider finding ways to use your strengths in social situations. For example, if you are a good listener, you might offer a listening ear to a friend in need. If you are creative, you might use your artistic skills to create something to share with others.

- **Seek constructive feedback from others**

Especially useful when your negative inner dialogue is nagging, constructive feedback can help you feel more confident and disprove any worst-case scenario you might be imagining.

What is constructive feedback anyway? Think of the last project you completed. Was it 100% perfect, or could you have improved anything? Constructive feedback is useful criticism that is meant to help you improve.

If you seek constructive feedback, be sure only to ask someone who is qualified to give it. Your teacher, for instance, or someone with expertise in the area you're asking about. If you got a B on a project, you could ask your teacher, "what could I have done better to make this an A+?"

Looking at this from the angle of social interaction, imagine you're with a close friend in a group of people you don't know well. You say something out of place, they laugh, then you feel awkward.

Seeking constructive feedback in this case would be asking your friend later on, "what did I say to make everyone laugh?" Maybe it's not what you said, but how you said it, or when you said it.

Maybe they laughed because it was genuinely funny, but you misinterpreted their response. Your friend can give you an outsider's perspective. If they're a true friend, they'll have your best interest at heart and tell you their honest opinion about how you can handle the situation better or interpret it more accurately next time.

Odds are your inner dialogue creates the worst possible imaginary story. Seeking constructive feedback gives you the chance to hear from someone qualified to give you advice. Not only that, but it gives you the tools to improve.

it's not about fixing a problem

Improving social skills is not about "fixing a problem" but rather about taking small steps toward more successful communication. It's important to remember that we aren't born with social skills, so we spend our lives developing and improving them over time with exposure to a variety of social situations.

key takeaways:

- Engaging in social situations can help to build confidence and improve social skills.
- Effective communication is a critical skill for building and maintaining relationships with others and is a key component of social skills.
- Embracing what makes us different and knowing our strengths can be an important step toward building self-confidence and improving social skills.
- Improving social skills is not necessarily about "fixing a problem" but rather about taking small steps toward more successful communication.

conclusion

Congratulations on taking the first step toward overcoming social anxiety! I hope you feel empowered with some new knowledge and tools to make your life easier and more fulfilling.

You now have a comprehensive guide filled with valuable insights, practical skills, and inspiring tips to help you build a thriving social life.

You now understand the nature of social anxiety. You have learned how to regulate your emotions, build confidence, and master your inner dialogue. You're well-equipped to face triggers with healthy coping skills. You've learned more about yourself, making it easier to find your people, and you have developed the right mindset to succeed.

By putting the information and techniques covered in this book into practice, you will take control of your inner world and put yourself on the path to lasting relief from social anxiety.

Keep up the great work, and never doubt for a second that you have the strength and resilience to lead a confident and fulfilling life.

thank you

Of all the other books you could have picked, you took a chance on this one.

I hope that, after reading this book, you are able to show yourself more compassion, understand your complex mind a little better, and that you have learned at least one thing that will allow you to thrive in ways you never have before.

Before you go, I wanted to ask you for one small favor. Could you please consider posting a review on amazon? This helps me to keep writing things my readers like, and helps other readers decide if this book is right for them.

You feedback has a direct influence on my next titles and it means the world to me.

Take care,

Jason

Get Your Bonus Ebook Stop Limiting Yourself

+ Free Small-talk Field Guide

+ 5 Simple Secrets of Great Communicators

Scan the QR code above to claim your free bonuses

————————OR————————

visit https://gifts-jasonforte.brokentiles.co/anxiety

Get Ready to Improve all your Conversations & Build Self-Confidence!

✔Five Simple Secrets of Great Communicators. Treat these tips as your bible to improve your communication skills.

✔Free e-book: Stop Limiting Yourself. Expert advice debunks the most common limiting beliefs and forces you to get out of your own head!

✔Printable Small-Talk Field Guide, including conversation topic inventory worksheet. Never be left with nothing to say, and learn to exit a conversation gracefully.

references

Child and Youth Well-being. (2020, July 23). "Sense of Belonging." Accessed on December 29 2022 from https://www.childyouthwellbeing.govt.nz/measuring-success/indicators/sense-belonging

Collins Amanda, (2021) "How to socialise when you have social anxiety" Retrieved from https://www.opencolleges.edu.au/blog/2016/07/04/mhm-socialise-social-anxiety/ Accessed on 20th December 2022

Cuncic, Arlin, (2020) "Situations That Can Trigger Anxiety" Retrieved from https://www.verywellmind.com/which-situations-trigger-anxiety-3024887 Accessed on 20th December 2022

Kessler, Ronald C. National Comorbidity Survey: Adolescent Supplement (NCS-A), 2001-2004. Inter-university Consortium for Political and Social Research [distributor], 2017-01-18. https://doi.org/10.3886/ICPSR28581.v6

Klaphaak, Adrian, (2022) "How to Identify Your Strengths and Weaknesses" Retrieved from https://www.wikihow.com/Identify-Your-Strengths-and-Weaknesses Accessed on 22nd December 2022

Mayo Clinic, (2022) "Social anxiety disorder (social phobia)" Retrieved from https://www.mayoclinic.org/diseases-conditions/social-anxiety-disorder/symptoms-causes/syc-20353561#:~:text=Emotional%20and%20behavioral%20symptoms&text=Worry%20about%20embarrassing%20or%20humiliating,or%20having%20a%20shaky%20voice Accessed on 16th December 2022

MBO Partners, (2022) "What Are Soft Skills? Why Soft Skills Are Important in the Workplace" Retrieved from https://www.mbopartners.com/blog/how-manage-small-business/why-are-soft-skills-important/#:~:text=Why%20are%20soft%20skills%20important,%2C%20attract%2C%20and%20retain%20clients. Accessed on 22nd December 2022

Melissa Kirk. "5 Ways to Find Your People (The Ones Who Really Get You)." Accessed on December 29 2022 from https://tinybuddha.com/blog/5-ways-find-your-people-the-ones-who-really-get-you/

Neff, K. (2015). In *Self-compassion: The proven power of being kind to yourself.* essay, William Morrow, an imprint of HarperCollinsPublishers.

Oro House Recovery Centers, (2022) "33 Famous People and Celebrities With Anxiety Disorders" Retrieved from https://www.ororecovery.com/9-famous-people-celebrities-with-social-anxiety-disorders/ Accessed on 15th December, 2022

Polaris teen Center, (2019) "SOCIAL ANXIETY IN TEENS: SIGNS, SYMPTOMS, AND HOW TO HELP" Retrieved from https://polaristeen.com/articles/social-anxiety-in-teens/ Accessed on 15th December, 2022

Raising Teens Today, (2021) "10 Important Social Skills You Need to Teach Your Teen Now" Retrieved from https://raisingteenstoday.com/10-important-social-skills-you-need-to-teach-your-teen-now/ Accessed on 15th December, 2022

Roncero, Alexia, (2021) "Automatic negative thoughts: how to identify and fix them"

Retrieved from https://www.betterup.com/blog/automatic-thoughts Accessed on 16th December 2022

Social Anxiety Disorder. (n.d.). National Institute of Mental Health (NIMH). https://www.nimh.nih.gov/health/statistics/social-anxiety-disorder

SkillsYouNeed, (2022) "Managing Your Internal Dialogue (Self-Dialogue)" Retrieved from https://www.skillsyouneed.com/ps/managing-self-dialogue.html Accessed on 20th December 2022

Waisman, Eric. (2022, October 27). "How to Build A Strong Social Circle in 5 Steps." Accessed on December 29 2022 from

https://www.jaunty.org/blog/how-to-build-a-strong-social-circle-in-5-steps

Walsh, Kathryn (2021) "Factors Affecting Self-Esteem in Teens" retrieved from https://healthfully.com/factors-affecting-self-esteem-in-teens-8702720.html Accessed on 21st December 2022

Witmer, Denise. (2020, May 23). "Teaching Your Teens to Use Their Manners." Accessed on December 29 2022 from https://www.verywellfamily.com/manners-your-teen-should-use-and-how-to-teach-them-2608864

Viktor Sander. (2022, April 8). "What is Social Circle?" Accessed on December 29 2022 from https://socialself.com/blog/social-circle-definition/

Made in United States
Troutdale, OR
09/28/2023

13265638R00058